EMOTIONAL REGULATION

FOR KIDS

30+ Fun Activities

To Build Positive Thinking, Self-Awareness, Social-Emotional Learning, Coping Techniques through CBT Exercises

By

JESICA MOSES

Disclaimer Notice

This book is written and published independently. Please keep in mind that the material in this publication is solely for educational and entertaining purposes. All efforts have provided authentic, up-to-date, trustworthy, and comprehensive information. There are no express or implied assurances. The purpose of this book's material is to assist readers in having a better understanding of the subject matter. The activities, information, and exercises are provided solely for self-help information. This book is not intended to replace expert psychologists, legal, financial, or other guidance. If you require counseling, please get in touch with a qualified professional. By reading this text, the reader accepts that the author will not be held liable for any damages, indirectly or directly, experienced due to the information included herein, particularly, but not limited to, omissions, errors, or inaccuracies. You are accountable for your decisions, actions, and consequences as a reader.

A LITTLE SOMETHING ABOUT ME

Readers, you are the best! I am Jesica Moses, your author and companion on your journey into the depths of your emotions; I am also the nefarious mind behind this fantastic experience. Please allow me to present myself.

I am a romantic idealist, a firm believer in the power of humor, and a sentimentalist at heart. I've spent a lot of time learning how to regulate my emotions after years of navigating the emotional landscape.

Even as a child, I experienced the emotional maelstrom that made me feel like a leaf in a storm. When I finally figured out how to control my feelings, though, amazing things began to happen. It was like unearthing a cache of happiness, fortitude, and a dash of silliness.

Every page is a labor of love, an invitation to embark on an adventure. I hope it will make you smile, think, and help you develop as a person. My goal is to give you the tools you need to ride out the emotional roller coaster with poise, humor, and self-assurance.

We're about to set sail on an adventure where humor will be the fuel that keeps us going and originality will be our rudder through choppy waters. My intention is simple: to bring a little enchantment into your life and provide you the means to star in your own emotional epic.

Put on your seatbelts, dear readers, and prepare to experience the full force of your extraordinary feelings. Let's go on this journey together, eyes wide open and spirits high.

With love, humor, and limitless creativity,
Your intrepid writer and fellow traveler!
-Jesica Moses

TABLE OF CONTENTS

SNEAK PEEK!

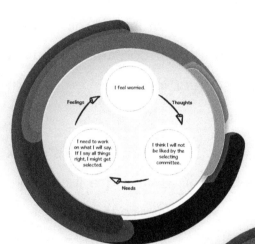

WELL...NOW WHAT?

The marvelous universe of "Emotions" awaits you, magnificent minds and fantastic pals! Are you prepared for an emotional roller coaster ride into a land of hilarity and zaniness? Get ready to use your incredible emotional talents, and fasten your seatbelts!

Here's a secret I want to convey to kids ages 9 to 12: emotions are like a box of chocolates. They come in a wide variety of forms and are incredibly tasty and entertaining. In this amazing booklet, we'll explore the marvelous world of emotional regulation in great detail. However, have no fear! This isn't just some meaningless jargon pulled from a textbook. We've concocted a potent potion of originality, tunefulness, and humor to turn your emotional trip into something truly out of the ordinary.

Think of a world where you can control your feelings much way a superhero controls their abilities. Yes, you heard me correctly; from here on out, you guys are going to rule the world when it comes to controlling your feelings. You will become an expert at riding the emotional waves, from the raging fires of rage to the euphoric surges of joy.

Inside these vivid pages, you'll find a goldmine of exercises that will make you laugh while teaching you to control your feelings. Get ready to be introduced to Captain Calm, your reliable companion on this journey. He'll lead you to inner peace using his ice cream super suit as a metaphor.

Get ready for an unprecedented adventure in the world of "Emotions"! As you scroll through this book, you'll find amusing cartoons, and thrilling games that are sure to have you entertained.

The story doesn't end there, though! The "Emotions" manual provides practical advice for dealing with challenging emotional situations. We'll show you how to still the roiling waves of anger, scale the dizzying heights of worry, and prance carefree through the sunshine of contentment.

Always keep in mind that feelings are allies, not enemies. And with the aid of "Emotions," you'll be the maestro of your own emotional symphony, composing a magnificent melody that will reverberate throughout your mind, body, and spirit.

Let's get our game faces on and charge full speed ahead into this thrilling experience. Where humor, originality, and emotional amazement meet is where "Emotions" can be found. It's time to release the immense power of your emotions and find your inner superhero.

Young heroes, I urge you to take this trip seriously since you are in for an emotional experience unlike any other. The world of "Emotions" awaits you!

It's time to start digging into your feelings.

CAMPAIGN A
(SELF AWARENESS)

Welcome to the first set of activities. The first phase of exercises in this book is specifically designed to acknowledge and accept all of your emotions. After all, how can you regulate something you don't fully know about? Think of this section as kind of a test run to let you know the basics. So, Let's get started!

HOW I FEEL?

This activity is a basic dive into how, what and why you feel certain emotions.

What to Do?

1. Look at the My Feelings worksheet.
2. Follow the instructions in the worksheet and fill it.

Profits of this activity:

1. By writing down your emotions and factors related to it, you will be more self-aware of your emotions and thoughts.
2. Expressing your thoughts and emotions allows you to shift your perspective and look into alternative possibilities.

MY FEELINGS

This is what I feel: _____

Happy	Angry	Upset	Proud
Anxious	Excited	Bored	Frightened
Irritated	Sad	Ill	Nervous

The reason I feel like this:

_____

_____

_____

How I managed it:

_____

_____

_____

Another path I could've taken:

_____

_____

_____

Asked for assistance	Did deep breathing	Walked away
Did something different	Informed my parents	Shared with a friend

THOUGHT UNRAVELING

This activity allows you to put your thoughts on paper and work around them to see more and better alternative thoughts.

What to Do?

1. Look at the Unraveling Thoughts worksheet.
2. Draw or write your thoughts in speech bubbles on the page.

Profits of this activity:

1. Encourages kids to think for themselves and think about what they are thinking.
2. They gain greater insight into the patterns of their thought as a result of participating in this activity.

UNRAVELING THOUGHTS

1. See the bubbles provided on the page?
2. In single bubbles, write one positive thought each.
3. In double bubbles, write a negative thought on one side and an alternative positive thought on the other side.

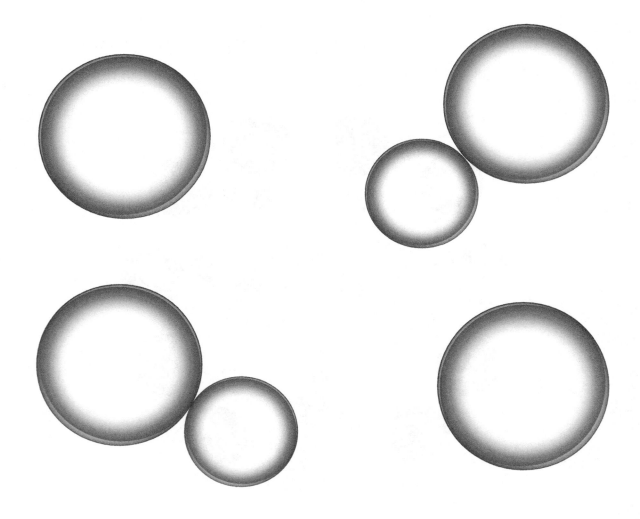

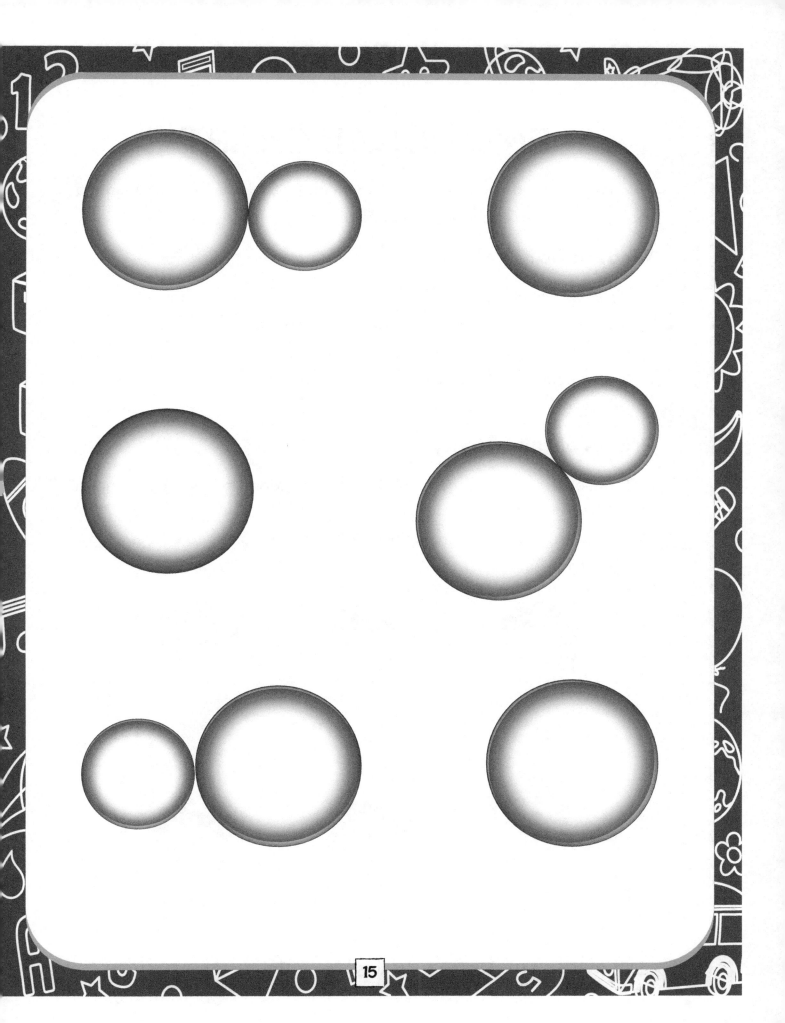

EMOTIONAL CHART

By combining visual perception with reflection, this activity allows kids to represent their emotions with the help of art.

What to Do?

1. Construct a chart of your own or make use of one that is already available, which includes a variety of facial expressions to represent different feelings.
2. In the course of the day, recognize and name the feelings you are experiencing.

Profits of this activity:

1. Emotional self-awareness will improve as a result of participating in this exercise.
2. It also helps in visual recognition skills when it comes to expressing or identifying emotions.

EXPRESSIVE LABELLING

1. See the different emojis below? Each represents what you feel.
2. Think of a moment when you were open about something to someone.
3. During that experience, which emotions you had, color them below and write why you felt that emotion beside it.

 _____

_____

 _____

_____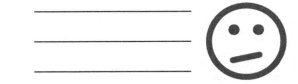

 _____

JOURNAL, JOURNAL

Hey kids! This journal is different than usual. How? In this activity you will write down your thoughts and feelings to secure them for your growth.

What to Do?

1. Keep a record of your thoughts and feelings.
2. Record your daily thoughts and feelings by either writing them down or drawing them.
3. Think about why you felt that way and what factors might have contributed to the development of those feelings.

Profits of this activity:

1. This pastime encourages introspection as well as an awareness of one's feelings.
2. Journaling your emotional or mental experiences helps you remember the good outcomes from those situations and you can use past or present experiences for future references.

ABILITIES COLLAGE

Sometimes known as "Strengths Collage" this activity is great for kids with low self-esteem or confidence. Kids will draw or write their strengths which will add to their emotional resilience.

What to Do?

1. Make a collage that illustrates the good attributes and strengths you have.
2. Use magazines to cut out words or photos, or draw what you consider to be your best qualities.
3. Look at the Strength Wall worksheet for guidance.

Profits of this activity:

1. Engaging in a conversation about one's singular attributes and the ways in which they contribute to the development of their sense of self and self-awareness.
2. Enhances art and craft skills.

STRENGTH WALL

1. A collage is given.
2. Write or draw your strengths in frames with answer lines.
3. Draw your strengths in blank frames.
4. Hidden talents are also welcome, they are strengths too! Don't be shy to collage them too.

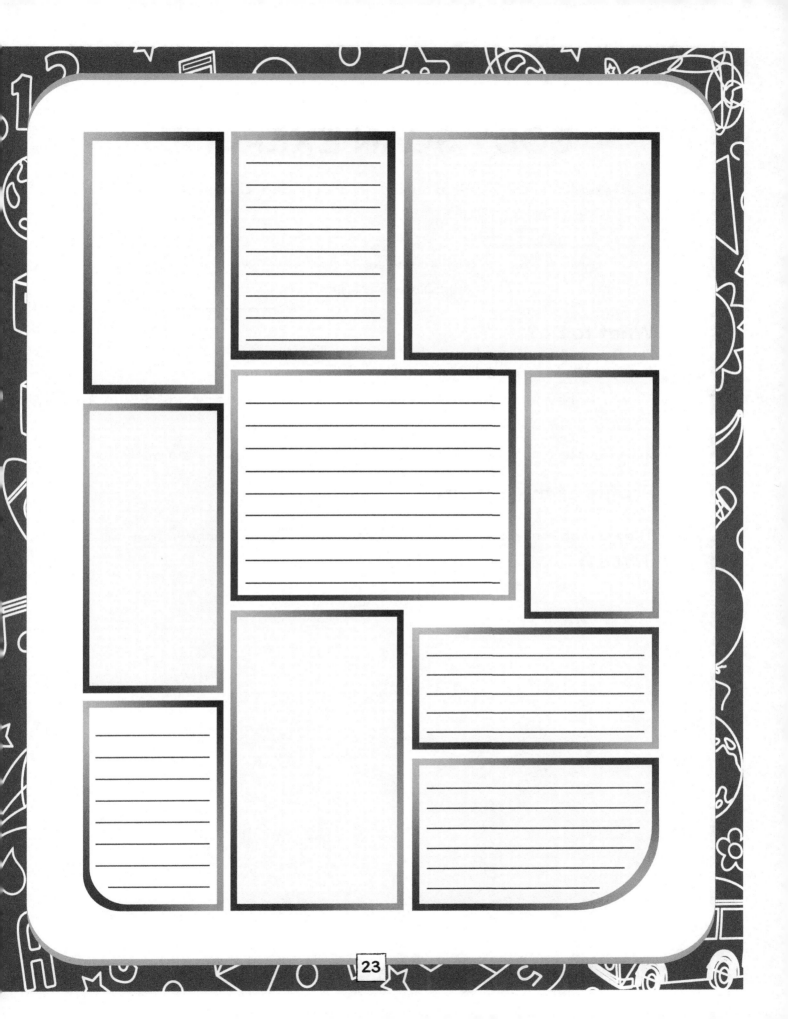

BODY SCAN EXERCISE

This exercise involves kids being in touch and connection with their mind-body connection.

This activity requires supervision from a parent, so run along kid and get your parent here before starting.

What to Do?

1. Help the kid by leading them through an exercise called a body scan, in which they focus their attention on every part of their body and make note of any sensations or feelings they experience.
2. A detailed instruction is given in the Mind-Body Exploration worksheet.

Profits of this activity:

They are able to gain a greater awareness of the link between their minds and bodies as a result of participating in this activity.

MIND-BODY EXPLORATION

Enlist the symptoms you feel on which body part and mark them on the images given.

_____   _____
_____   _____
_____   _____
_____   _____
_____   _____

Front:

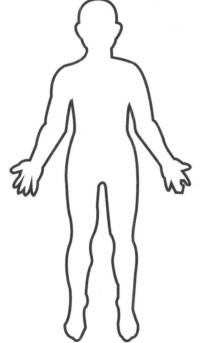

Back:

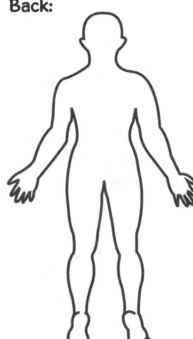

Write down all the possible sources or causes that you know or suspect are causing stress in the marked body parts? How is it affecting you emotionally?

_____
_____
_____
_____
_____
_____
_____

Suggest to yourself healthy coping mechanisms to avoid stress that causing symptoms in your body.

_____
_____
_____

MY FEARS

It is difficult sometimes to face one's fears but it is the only way to move forward. This activity helps you do just that.

What to Do?

1. Look at the Out with My Fears worksheet.
2. Fill the worksheet as asked.

Profits of this activity:

1. Accepting and acknowledging one's fears is one step to identifying the underlying emotions that are root cause of the fears.
2. Good emotions that are erratic or are being blocked by fears and nervousness can be brought into light.

OUT WITH MY FEARS

Write the things that make you feel nervous or scared.

_____
_____
_____

What is the first thought that comes to your mind when you feel scared?

_____
_____

Mark the areas of your body where fear affects you the most.

What can you do something to feel better next time you are afraid?

_____
_____

GRIEF COMPLETION

> *You don't have to do this activity right away if you feel it's much for you. Keep it for later for when you feel better to do this.*

What to Do?

1. Look at the Sorrow Completion worksheet.
2. Fill the worksheet by answering the questions.

Profits of this activity:

1. Talking about loss, grief etc. is difficult to talk about, but it is important to acknowledge and accept them along with positive aspects in life.
2. By accepting and coming to terms with loss and grief you have faced, you can feel lightened from the burden and move towards better recovery.

SORROW COMPLETION

At this moment, I feel: _____
_____

I am the saddest when: _____
_____

What I miss about the person I have lost:
_____

Things have been different since I lost that person because:
_____
_____

Current emotional status of my family:
_____

The one last thing I could ask from the person I lost would be:
_____
_____

Things I liked most about that person were:
_____

The one important life lesson that person taught me was:
_____
_____

SELF-CARE

Self-care is all about management. This activity lets kids create managemental skills for their self-care. Self-care nourishes emotional health.

What to Do?

1. Practice healthy habits, such as getting enough amount of sleep, eating meals high in nutrients, and maintain good cleanliness.
2. Positive Affirmations: Inspire children to engage in positive self-talk by utilizing affirmations and give them opportunities to do so.

Profits of this activity:

1. Healthy habits not only improve one's health as a whole but also have the potential to positively influence emotional regulation by providing introspection.
2. In order to build one's self-esteem and cultivate a resilient mindset, you could instruct utter positive words about yourselves.

EMOTIONS PORRIDGE

Goldilocks is not the only one with the porridge case.

This activity allows kids to assess objectively what their emotions are made of.

What to Do?

1. Look at the Emolock's Porridge worksheet.
2. Fill the bowl by following the given instructions.

Profits of this activity:

1. This activity allows you to look at your emotions from an objective perspective.
2. By identifying how one or a collection of your emotions are made from what and how many constituents, you will be able to better understand them and therefore, manage them accordingly.

FEELYLOCK'S PORRIDGE

In the feelings porridge add ingredients you believe make the recipe for your emotions.

Recipe:

TFN (THOUGHTS FEELINGS NEEDS)

By understanding patterns of thoughts, feelings and needs and how they are correlated, kids can effectively manage their emotions and life style.

What to Do?

1. Look at the Correlations worksheet.
2. Fill out according the given instructions.

Profits of this activity:

1. Our thoughts, feelings, behaviors and needs are all interconnected in life.
2. By identifying what and how one factor ties in with the other, you can express yourself better since you become better aware of your personality traits.

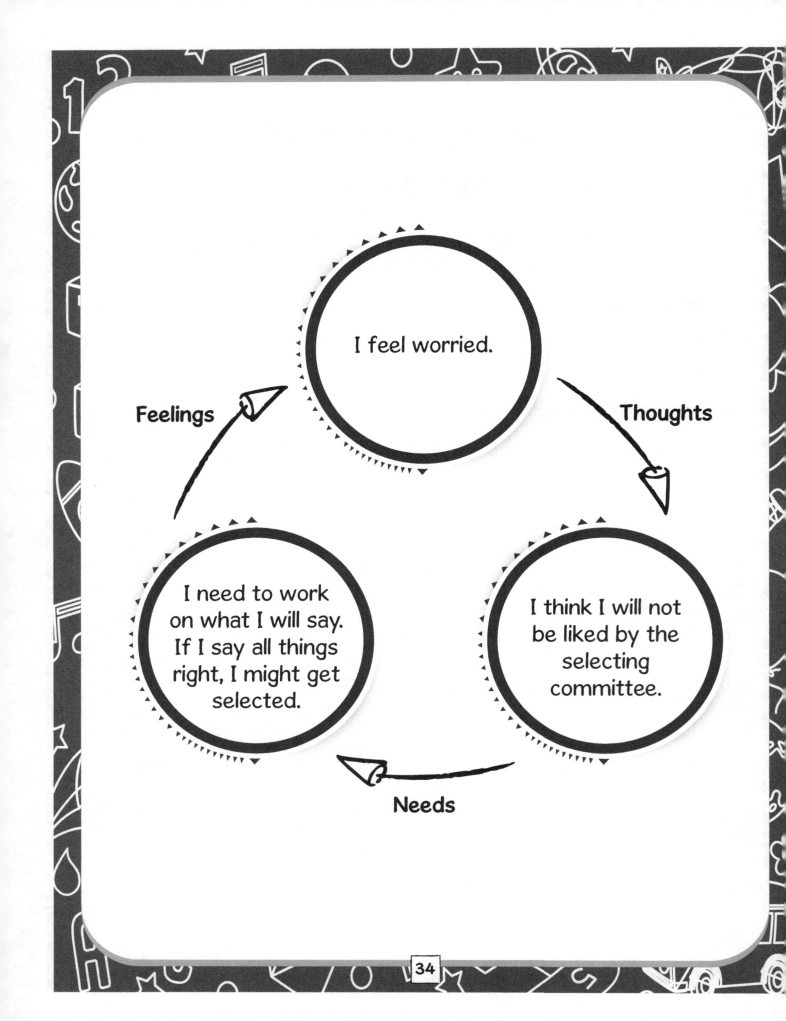

I feel worried.

Feelings

Thoughts

I need to work on what I will say. If I say all things right, I might get selected.

I think I will not be liked by the selecting committee.

Needs

CAMPAIGN B
(SOCIAL-EMOTIONAL LEARNING)

The second phase of our journey advances to a slightly higher level of emotional development through the use of a social outlook. Think of this part of activities as a combined learning experience. Some activities you will do alone but most will be in the form of groups. You may need a team in this campaign often times.

I would like to address to the parents as well here to be involved in this section of the book.

THOUGHT TRAFFIC WARDEN

These are the kind of parking tickets everyone should receive. This activity allows kids to stop unwanted negative thoughts on command.

What to Do?

1. Draw a red light whenever you have an unhelpful or negative thought.
2. Draw a green light, to represent constructive and advantageous ideas.
3. Draw an orange image when you have successfully converted a negative thought into a positive one.
4. Ask someone, a parent or to friend to draw a colored signal according to what thought or feeling you had. You can also draw the traffic lights yourself.

Profits of this activity:

1. Encourages the person to "stop" thinking negatively and suggest that they think on something good instead.
2. Gives the kid a sense of diversion to sway away from the negative aspects.

EMOTIONAL TRAFFIC LIGHTS

The analogy of traffic lights is a useful tool for teaching you to notice and take control of your thoughts.

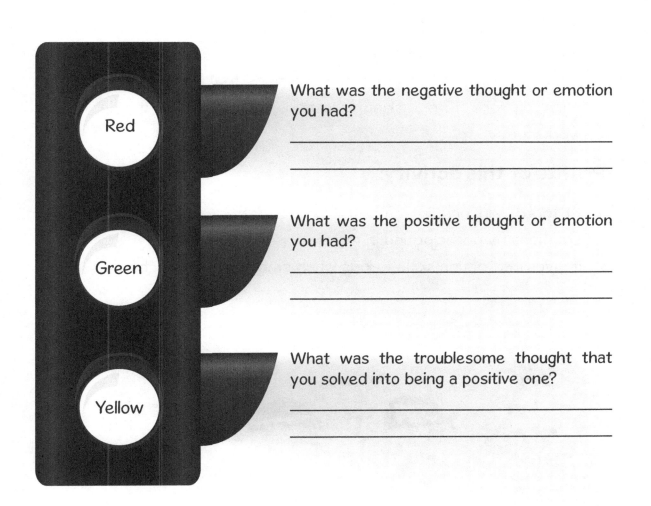

What was the negative thought or emotion you had?

_____

_____

What was the positive thought or emotion you had?

_____

_____

What was the troublesome thought that you solved into being a positive one?

_____

_____

FEELING CHARADES

Role-playing emotions allows kids to learn and understand emotions better because they gain an outside perspective and understanding.

Note: This is a group activity, so I suggest you get yourself some partners.

What to Do?

1. Act out a game of charades in which you must not speak while portraying a variety of feelings.
2. Hold a discussion regarding the emotions that were expressed after each player's turn, asking questions as shown in the Inside Out worksheet.

Profits of this activity:

1. Children can acquire empathy and a better understanding of their emotions by participating in this exercise.
2. It gives interaction skills to kids when emotions are concerned.

INSIDE OUT

"How did you know what emotion they were expressing?"

_____

_____

_____

_____

"When have you felt that emotion before?"

_____

_____

_____

_____

What emotions deeply resonated with you?

_____

_____

_____

_____

PROBLEM SOLVING PROMPTS

Giving kids scenarios to solve and resolve helps them tap into their inner selves and relate their emotional health with the situation at hand.

> *Alert: Another group activity, go find yourself a team!*
> *I recommend adults and other kids.*

What to Do? (For Parents/Adults)

1. Children should be given scenarios that challenge them to use their problem-solving skills.
2. They should work in pairs or small groups.
3. Give them the scenarios, and have them act them out while trying to come up with constructive solutions.
4. After that, have a conversation about the various solutions and urge people to think about tactics that are useful for resolving issues.

Profits of this activity:

1. Problem-solving activities help kids overcome obstacles. These experiences teach them resilience, perseverance, and that setbacks are part of problem-solving.
2. Problem-solving sometimes involves considering others' needs. Children gain empathy, understanding, and social responsibility. Emotional intelligence and empathy are developed.
3. Adaptability and flexibility: Problem-solving activities often require youngsters to modify their strategies and approaches to feedback and changing conditions. This helps them adapt to unforeseen situations and think creatively.
4. Self-confidence and empowerment: Solving issues inspires youngsters. It boosts confidence and shows they can conquer obstacles. This confidence boosts self-esteem.

GROUP ART PROJECT

This activity gives kids free reign on how they create graphic narrative of their emotional experiences.

Note: You guessed it! Another group activity, hope you have your squad assembled?

What to Do? (For Parents/Kids)

1. Ask the children to sketch a map of their daily routine on a large sheet of paper or a whiteboard that you have provided to them.
2. Tell them to add places and things that they have any emotional connection within their daily lives.
3. Instruct them to identify and name the various emotional states that experience, as well as the situations or triggers that cause those emotions to rise.

Profits of this activity:

1. This exercise helps participants become more self-aware and gain a better understanding of their inner selves.
2. Greatly enhances self-expression skills, which are core factors for self-awareness.

FRIENDSHIP COLLAGE

In this activity, kids can get a chance to practice skills and emotional criteria related to making friends.

Alert: Yep! You know the drill…

What to Do? (For Parents/Kids)

1. Instruct the children to construct a collage that illustrates the attributes they look for in a friend and the characteristics they bring to a friendship.

2. They can illustrate their thoughts by drawing, cutting out pictures or sentences from magazines, or combination of both.

Profits of this activity:

1. Starts a conversation about the significance of positive relationships and how these characteristics contribute to the development of healthy friendships.

2. Instills self-confidence in kids, which is required for being social. Self-confidence also boosts self-awareness and self-expression.

MYSTERY SOLVE N' ESCAPE GAME

Through this fun exercise, kids can develop their mental and emotional well-being by overcoming obstacles and striving for achievement. It offers an invaluable opportunity for growth and practice.

> *You're gonna need your squad here. So, assemble!*

What to Do? (For Parents/Kids)

1. Create a mystery-solving game in which players must investigate clues to find the locations of a missing person.
2. As you make you way farther into the game, you may be confronted with a variety of mental obstacles, such as irritation or disappointment when it is difficult to uncover clues.
3. Create a situation in which you can take on the roles of detectives or even imposters and work together or work against to solve or sabotage a mystery.
4. You can simulate an escape room either at home or in a specifically designed location.
5. It's possible that you will experience periods of frustration, bewilderment, or exhilaration as you work together to solve puzzles and uncover the mystery.

Profits of this activity:

1. In order to continue playing the game, encourage them to appropriately handle the emotions they are experiencing.
2. Incorporate, at various points during the game, events that trigger a variety of feelings, such as the discovery of an unexpected hint or the encountering of an unexpected obstacle.

3. Encourage children to talk about and take control of their feelings while they are playing the game.

4. Encourages connection and teamwork among participants as they discover how to control their emotions and collaborate to conquer challenges.

COLLECTIVE STORY BOARD

Having different stories of different people can give a person a more diverse sense of situations and experiences in life.

Note: Team up with others who have stories to tell.

What to Do? (For Parents/Kids)

1. Read or create stories that highlight different perspectives and emotions.
2. Each kid can either create an original short story or write a part of a bigger overall story for the group.
3. After everyone has written their stories, they can all paste it on a board, much like the image I have shown.
4. After reading the stories, engage children in a discussion about how characters might have felt and why.

Profits of this activity:

1. Encourages kids to consider alternative viewpoints and practice empathy.
2. It allows kids to foster cooperation and sharing skills.

MY STORY BOARD

CREATE YOUR LARP

Gaming on the field? I got you. This exercise allows kids to use their imagination and get creative while facing opportunities to emotionally grow in a narrative sequence.

What to Do? (For Parents/Kids)

1. Look at the Gamer's Realm Worksheet.
2. Fill out the worksheet, following the instructions provided.
3. Once you have created the requirements from the worksheet, it is important you actually role play by choosing a suitable story, universe and plot twists.
4. Have fun!

Profits of this activity:

1. LARP worksheets allow kids to work together. While creating and performing their roles, they can practice communication, negotiation, collaboration, and conflict resolution.
2. LARPing can help kids develop emotional intelligence by letting them play different characters and experience different emotions in a safe atmosphere. They can comprehend and control their emotions and sympathize with others.
3. Complex LARP worksheets require critical thinking and decision-making. Children must evaluate facts and make decisions that affect their characters and the plot. This improves problem-solving and critical thinking.

Choose your Species/Faction

Earth Magic Warlocks

Air Telekinesis Fairies

Fire Pyromancy Valkyrie

Water Teleportation Nymphs

Void Mind Reading Villia

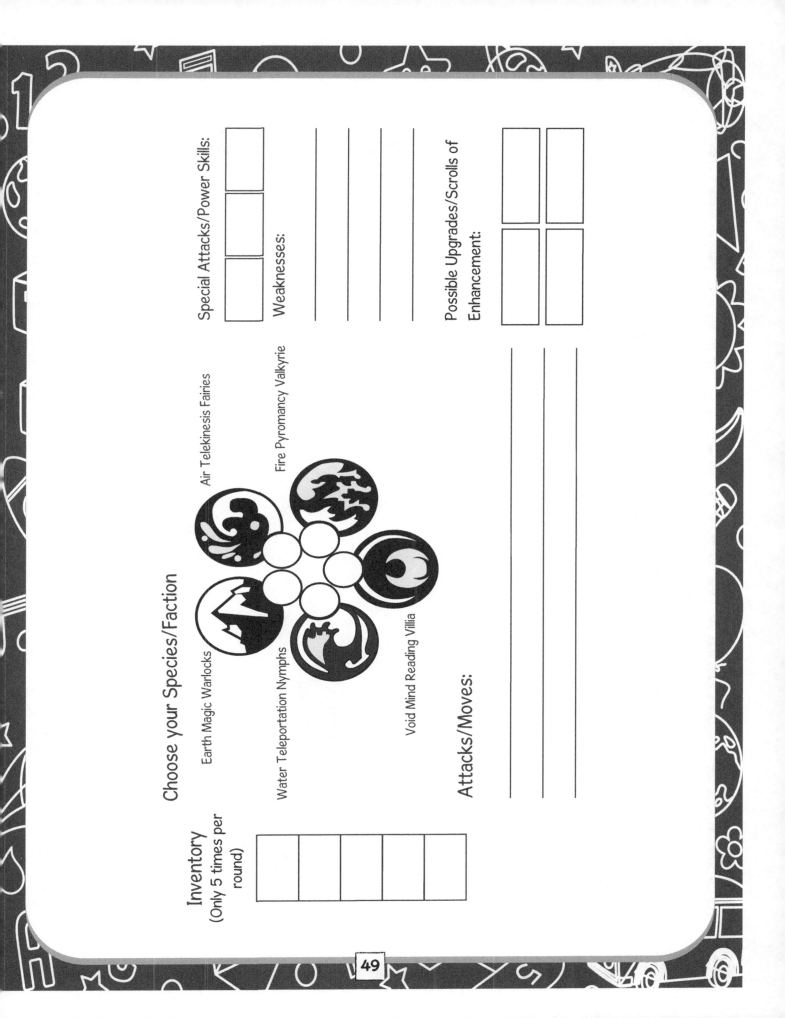

Special Attacks/Power Skills:

Weaknesses:

_____

_____

_____

Possible Upgrades/Scrolls of
Enhancement:

_____

_____

_____

Attacks/Moves:

_____

_____

_____

Inventory
(Only 5 times per
round)

FEELING CARDS

This activity allows kids to be spontaneous and share their life stories when working in a group.

> *This activity is best done in a group, so gather your friends.*
> *Note: Parents should help and supervise this activity.*

What to Do? (For Parents/Kids)

1. Create a set of emotion cards featuring a variety of distinct facial expressions to represent the many types of emotions.
2. After shuffling them, lay the cards out on a table with the backs down.
3. The children take it in turns to select a card and then discuss a personal event that is connected to that feeling.

Profits of this activity:

1. This activity enables participants to reflect on their own feelings.
2. Develop empathy for others.
3. Improve their communication skills.

EMOTIONAL SOLITAIRE

POTLUCK

Who does not like food? But it is always better to eat with people. This activity promotes It is important for kids to learn the concepts of give and take; sharing.

What to Do? (For Parents/Kids)

1. You can host a potluck or you can plan to go to a potluck you are invited to.
2. Assign each family member an appetizer, main entrée, side dish, dessert, or beverage. Keep options balanced.
3. Ask family members to print or share their recipes. This can start discussions on food, cooking, and culture.
4. Give each family member a place to exhibit their cuisine. Label dishes and families on tables or buffets.
5. Let other kids try what you have brought. Provide sample plates and utensils. Encourage them to experiment and share their opinions.
6. Make sure to clean and help later after the event is finished.

Profits of this activity:

1. Children develop social and communication skills.
2. This activity instills a sense of community and volunteer ship.
3. By sharing experiences, opinions and feelings through food related activities, children can develop skills of emotional management and regulation.

NOT SO ALONE KIDDO.
(REAL LIFE EXAMPLE OF KID WHO HAD THEIR EMOTIONAL HEALTH REGULATED THROUGH THESE EXERCISES)

Once upon a time, there was a lively and inquisitive young man named Alex who lived in a bustling city. Alex had a heart as vast as the universe, yet their feelings were often unpredictable. One day, Alex discovered about CBT (Cognitive Behavioral Therapy) which led him to this book and today here I am narrating his story.

Alex's anticipation for this journey of self-discovery was palpable as he enthusiastically dove into the bright pages. Alex learned the incredible strength of deep breathing in the first exercise. Alex could now control their rage whenever it erupted like a volcano in their veins. Alex learnt to calm his raging emotions by breathing deeply, just like a dragon.

The next thing Alex saw was a fantastic comic strip adventure that had valuable lessons about naming emotions. They learned through humorous cartoons that the mind can play tricks on the emotions. With this new information at their disposal, Alex set about unraveling their inner workings, much like a sleuthing Sherlock Holmes.

Alex's life changed drastically, though, when he discovered a remarkable game called "The Emotional Orchestra." Like a symphony's conductor, it forced them to coordinate their feelings with calming coping mechanisms. Alex's EQ improved dramatically with each harmonious pairing. They overcame their fears by summoning their courage, and they found relief from their sorrows by listening to music or receiving a comforting embrace.

Alex's ability to control his emotions grew like a beautiful flower over the course of several weeks. When their loved ones saw the changes, they naturally turned to Alex for guidance. They taught others the benefits of accepting and experiencing their feelings without judgment.

Over time, Alex came to understand that these CBT activity books were more than simply books; they were entryways to a universe where resiliency in the face of emotional hardship was attainable for anyone. Alex felt such profound gratitude that he decided to share the miracle of self-control with the world.

Alex took the platform before an adoring audience years later to talk about his or her extraordinary adventure to find oneself. Alex's transformation into an inspirational role model, illuminating the road to mental health using CBT activity books, is a testament to their efficacy.

As a result, many people found hope in Alex's experience, a child who learned to control his emotions with the use of cognitive behavioral therapy (CBT) activity books. Each page turned revealed a fresh hero, eager to face their inner demons and live life to the fullest.

CAMPAIGN C
(POSITIVE THINKING)

The third phase of our journey involves exercises to foster positivity in you through and through. The activities in this section are simple yet effective, promoting emotional resilience when done honestly and frequently in a week.

POSITIVE VISUALIZATION

This activity gives kids a chance to reflect on their experiences and stop negative thoughts using cues. It builds emotional resilience.

What to Do?

1. Visualize by imagining a situation in your mind. This situation must be one where you strived to achieve the positive outcome.
2. Notice disruptive or unhelpful thoughts and interrupt those ideas with a physical or verbal cue.
3. You could, for instance, verbally exclaim "Stop!" or snap your fingers in order to stop the pattern of negative thinking.
4. Fill out the Aftermath worksheet below after doing the activity.

Profits of this activity:

1. This activity allows kids to block things that may disrupt when they are in a state of emotional positivity.
2. It also builds the sense to develop boundaries to avoid adverse situations.

AFTERMATH

What was the situation that you imagined?

_____

_____

_____

What did you do to attain positivity in this moment?

_____

_____

_____

What were the bad thoughts or feelings that went through you during this moment?

_____

_____

_____

What valuable lesson have you learned?

_____

_____

_____

_____

TALK TO YOURSELF

It is crucial for people to acknowledge and take care of their mental and emotional needs while we work to promote a positive attitude. Speaking to oneself can help you shape your thoughts and feelings.

What to Do?

1. Confront negative ideas and exchange them with constructive and realistic self-talk by encouraging yourself to do so.
2. Look at the Reframing Thoughts worksheet.

Profits of this activity:

1. Rearranging negative thoughts helps kids become more optimistic. Kids can improve their emotional well-being and minimize unhappiness, worry, and frustration by challenging harmful beliefs and replacing them with good, realistic ones.
2. Reframing negative beliefs teaches kids resilience and coping skills. They become more optimistic and develop excellent coping mechanisms.
3. Negative thoughts can stress kids out. Reframing these attitudes reduces stress by encouraging a more positive and adaptable reaction to difficult events. It helps kids manage stress.
4. Reframing negative beliefs helps kids become more cheerful and positive. This increases life satisfaction, pleasure, and well-being.

REFRAMING THOUGHTS

In the negative clouds, write negative feelings or thoughts, next to it in the positive cloud, write an alternative positive feeling or thought.

For instance, if you are feeling concerned about an upcoming test, for instance, you can reframe your thoughts by encouraging yourself to say something along the lines of "I have been studying and ready, so I will do my best."

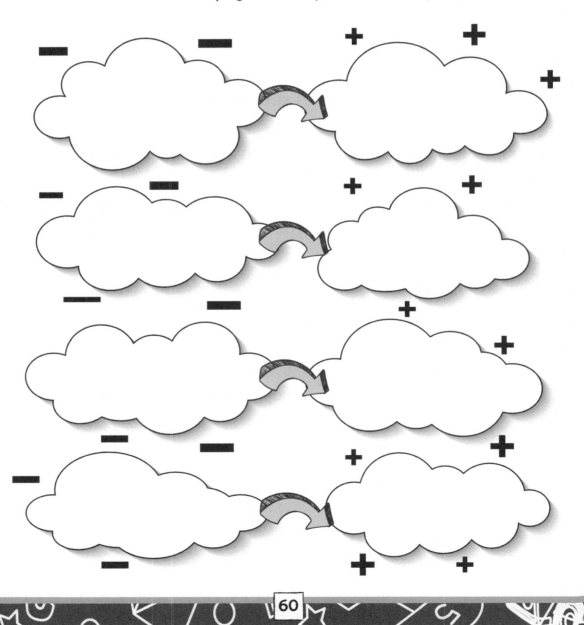

SINGING OUT GOODNESS

Art, specifically music and singing, is a great way to get your emotions regulated in a healthy and productive manner. It gives them a platform for self-expression and enables them to express happy emotions through composing songs.

What to Do?

1. Create song lyrics and then compose a song. What positive feeling do you want to convey through the song? That's up to you.
2. Lyrics don't have to sound professional or adhere to any certain formula. The only rule is to write honestly.
3. After finishing the song's words and music, you can perform it for yourself or with someone special. They can also provide musical accompaniment.
4. Discuss the thoughts and feelings that inspired the song's lyrical content and musical arrangement after each performance.

Profits of this activity:

1. Kids can benefit from songwriting because it gives them a safe way to communicate their feelings.
2. Capabilities like self-regulation and constructive social interaction are bolstered.
3. Putting emphasis on your positive emotions and thoughts will help others relate to them.

POSITIVE MOMENTS IN LIFE

Remembering the awesome days that have happened in your life is important. It provides an escape from stress and gives you insight into possible solutions for a current problem.

What to Do?

1. Look at the "The Good Days of My Life" worksheet.
2. Follow the instructions in the worksheet.

Profits of this activity:

1. Thinking about positive events in life from the past or recent present can bring peace of mind when a negative emotion is disturbing kids.
2. This activity also helps in jogging memory, remembering important details from past events that are crucial to present circumstances.

THE GOOD DAYS OF MY LIFE

Shoot the memory bullets you see below. But wait! Load them with gunpowder first. That gunpowder is positive memories from good days of your life.

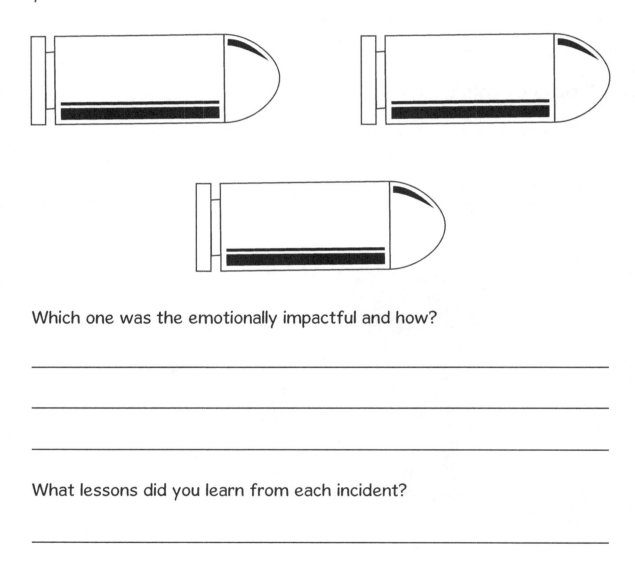

Which one was the emotionally impactful and how?

_____

_____

_____

What lessons did you learn from each incident?

_____

_____

_____

PICK YOUR ROLE MODELS

Having someone to look up to is no easy feat. This activity is here to change that. It is important for kids to idolize or be inspired by a person. This helps in any personality traits through introspection.

What to Do?

1. Look at the "The One I Look Upto" worksheet.
2. Write a short essay according to the instructions, describing the role model you admire and why they motivate you.

Profits of this activity:

1. Role models exhibit honesty, integrity, perseverance, and compassion. Children can develop their morals and become well-rounded by witnessing and imitating these traits.
2. Positive role models help kids believe in themselves and witness achievement. They increase self-esteem and resilience.
3. Kids often imitate others. Positive role models can encourage healthy habits, responsible decision-making, and social skills and consequently provide a better and healthier emotional health.

CAMPAIGN D
(COPING TECHNIQUES)

A coping mechanism is any decision, conscious or unconscious, that an individual makes in order to alleviate or console themselves when they are confronted with a stressful situation. That being said, we are in the final phase of our journey; the activities in the final phase are more like techniques that will help you cope with irregular emotions or thoughts in times of distress.

SOCIAL SUPPORT

An additional resource that can prove to be highly valuable is a support system. You have the ability to talk to other people who have actually experienced the same kind of emotional experience that you are going through, so they can understand what you are going through. People who have successfully moved on from distressing experiences are likely to be part of a support group alongside individuals who are still grappling with the aftereffects of the traumatic incident. There is a significant likelihood that these individuals will be there.

What to Do?

1. When you are going through tough times, it is important to reach out for support from dependable friends, family members, or mentors.
2. Do not shy away from texting or calling someone you wish to interact with when you are going through an emotionally troubling time.

Profits of this activity:

Teach kids how to effectively communicate with others and how to articulate their sentiments and requirements to those around them.

GROUNDING TECHNIQUES

The term "grounding" refers to a collection of straightforward techniques that might assist you in distancing yourself from unpleasant feelings (such as worry, anger, depression, or thoughts of harming yourself). Simply said, it is a strategy for diverting your attention away from the challenging feelings that you are going through by concentrating on anything else.

Grounding has many techniques, but the one will be easy for you to do is the "Visualization Technique".

What to Do?

Look at the "Grounding Yourself in Reality" handout worksheet.

Profits of this activity:

1. Grounding tactics like visualization and the senses of sight, sound, and smell can distract you from overwhelming emotions and ideas.
2. Emotional Irregularity and traumatic flashbacks can cloud judgment. Grounding practices, which entail focusing on the present, might help you calm your mind and body.

VISUALIZATION TECHNIQUE

- **Imagining You've Escaped Your Agony**

You can run, swim, or ride away from unpleasant emotions by treating your thoughts as a song or TV show you detest and either changing the channel or turning down the volume. Taking stock of one's feelings and packing them up in a cylinder.

- **Think About Someone You Care About**

Picture having someone who understands and is there for you anytime you're feeling down. Imagine their appearance or attempt to hear their voice in your head. Just picture them telling you that they know you'll make it through this tough time.

PROGRESSIVE MUSCLE RELAXATION

Children should be led through a progressive muscle relaxation practice, in which different muscular groups in their bodies are tensed and then relaxed, one after the other.

Note: This activity requires adult or parental supervision.

What to Do?

1. Look at the worksheet handout below by the name of "Physical Therapy".
2. Follow the instructions in it accordingly.

Profits of this activity:

This method encourages relaxation and lowers levels of physical tension in the body.

PHYSICAL THERAPY

• Arms and Hands

Imagine you have a whole lemon in your left hand, and you are about to squeeze it. Pull down firmly. Attempt to extract as much flavor as possible. Squeeze as hard as you can and feel the strain in your hand and arm. Put down the lemon and take it easy. Try loosening up your hand and seeing how much better it feels. Switch hands and do it again.

• Shoulders and Arms

Think of yourself as a fluffy, unproductive cat. A stretch is what you need. Raise your arms in front of you at shoulder height. Put them much above your head. Years ago. You should feel a tug at the shoulders. Elevate your stance. Relax and return your arms to your sides. Cat, please stretch out once more. Repeat.

• Neck and Shoulder

Imagine you're a turtle for a moment. You're basking in the sunshine on a rock next to a tranquil pond. It's comfortable, cozy, and secure in here. Oh-Oh! You are alerted to impending peril. Bring your thoughts inside. Attempt to bring your shoulder blades up to your ears and down into your cranium. Don't panic. It's tough being a turtle stuck inside its shell. The threat is no longer present. You can return to the comforting warmth of the sun and the open air. Be careful now. Increased peril. Quick, go back inside and keep your head down. Repeat.

- **Jaw**

A huge piece of jawbreaker bubble gum has found its way into your mouth. Extremely tough chewing. Use your teeth. Hard! Make use of the muscle tissue in your neck. Here, unwind. Don't worry about holding back your jaw. Take note of how relieving it is to let your jaw drop. Let's go back and try to crack that tough nut. Repeat.

- **Nose and Face**

A fly has just landed on the window. He fell squarely on your nostril. Don't use your hands if you can help it. Yes, make a wrinkle in the bridge of your nose. Create as many creases as possible in your nose. Pull your nose up and in tightly. Good. You managed to scare him off. Your nostrils may finally unwind. Oh my, here he is again. Repeat.

- **Stomach**

Hey! A newborn elephant is coming up the path. But he isn't paying attention to his surroundings. He's going to walk on your stomach since he can't see you laying in the grass. Stay put. You can't move out of the path right now. Prepare yourself for him. Try to harden your stomach. Contract your ab muscles as tightly as you can. Don't go just yet. It seems he is taking a different route. You can finally unwind. Give in to a weak stomach. Keep things as chill as possible. That's a huge relief. I didn't see him coming back this way. Preparation is key. Repeat.

- **Limbs and Footwear**

Imagine you have no shoes on and are standing in a large puddle of mud. Dig your toes in the mud as much as you can. Make an effort to sink your toes into the mud. Feel the muck squishing up between your toes as you press down and stretch them apart. Get your feet out of that puddle of muck. Put your feet up and chill out. Feel the pleasant freedom that comes from letting your toes dangle. Being at ease is a wonderful feeling. Repeat...

DEEP BREATHING

A method for relieving stress in which the practitioner is instructed to concentrate on taking long, calm breaths. In order to help relieve tension, discomfort, and anxiety, deep breathing is a technique that can be performed. This type of breathing is also referred to as "Belly Breathing" or "Diaphragmatic Breathing".

There are numerous deep breathing techniques, but here I will describe two for you.

What to Do?

1. **Breathing Like a Feather**

   One of my personal favorites for instructing children on how to properly breathe is to use feathers.

— **How to:**

1. Gather together feathers of a variety of colors.
2. Instruct your youngster to take the feather in their hand and hold it there.
3. Take a few full breaths in here. (Show your child how to do this first) If you want to teach children how to take a full breath, have them put their hands on their stomachs and feel the rise and fall of their stomach as they breathe deeply.
4. Take a deep breath and count to five as you.
5. The next step is to carefully exhale through the nose, and while you do so, softly blow up one side of the feather and down the other side while you are exhaling.

2. Flower Breathing

— How to:

1. Gather a flower, or have your child think of their favorite flower as if they have collected.
2. Instruct your youngster to take many deep breaths, and while they are doing so, take a LARGE whiff of the fragrant flower.
3. Count to ten while you don't breathe for it.
4. Hold your breath while you count to ten while exhaling through your mouth.
5. Keep doing this for the next five minutes.

Profits of this activity:

Teach children to help them calm their bodies and minds in times of stress and to cope with emotional disturbances.

MINDFULNESS TASK

Your mental and physical health will benefit from practicing mindfulness, and it may even make you happier overall. Below I have described some common, easy and effective mindfulness tasks.

Note: This last section is only for parents to read, but you can read to kiddos, just make sure you do practice these tasks!

What to Do?

1. **Exploration of the Five Senses**

   Instruct children to investigate their local surroundings by using all five of their senses. You should inquire them to take note of five things they can see, four things they can touch, three things they can hear, two things they can smell, and one item they can taste.

2. **Walking Mindfully**

   Accompany your children on a brisk stroll while reminding them to focus their attention on each step they take. Ask them to pay attention to the feeling of their feet making contact with the ground, the movement of their legs, as well as the sounds and things that are occurring around them.

3. **Mindful Eating**

   Ask the children to choose out a bite-sized piece of food for themselves, such as a raisin or a slice of fruit. Encourage children to pay close attention to the meal by asking them to take note of its color, fragrance, and texture. Encourage them to taste the flavors by taking little bites and paying attention to each feeling as they chew and swallow as you do so.

4. Mindful Listening

Playing kids' favorite music or sounds from nature might help them develop the skill of careful listening. Give them the instruction to close their eyes and concentrate on the noises, encouraging them to pay attention to the varying tones, rhythms, and patterns. Encourage them to empty their minds of all thoughts and focus just on the sensations that their ears are experiencing.

5. Mindful Coloring

Coloring attentively involves giving children coloring pages and asking them to color while paying attention to the strokes they make, the colors they select, and the sensations of the crayons or markers in their hands. This is an activity that falls under the category of mindful coloring. Inspire them to participate in the creative process with their full selves.

Profits of this activity:

1. The practice of mindfulness can be extremely useful for children, as it can help improve their mental health, concentration, and ability to self-regulate their emotions.
2. Kids can benefit from regular practice of mindfulness activities, which can help them develop self-awareness, the ability to regulate their emotions, focus, and overall well-being.

YOU HAVE THE POWER

It's time to say goodbye to my fantastic buddies as we conclude our extraordinary journey into the realm of emotions. But have no fear; the power to control your emotions will always be within your reach. It's time to wrap up our crazy adventure, so let's look back on all the awesome abilities you have discovered and all the good times we had together.

You, yes YOU, have conquered your feelings; you rule the emotional world! Do you recall a time when irritation attempted to make you snap? You high-fived it and said, "Not today, buddy!" in a hushed tone. Concern, too? It has finally learned to relax whenever it is with you. You have experienced the full range of human emotion, from joyful dancing to navigating the labyrinth of despair to scaling the heights of fear.

This zany journey has taught you that your feelings are like a palette of vibrant paints, just waiting to be used to create masterpieces out of your everyday experiences. All of your feelings are important and add something special to your experience. All the happy, sad, nervous, and giddy times that make your heart soar should be welcomed with open arms.

But keep in mind, dear friends, that learning to control your emotions is more than a one-time exercise. As you mature, you will feel new emotions and confront new obstacles, and it is in these moments that your resiliency will be tested. With the knowledge you've gained from this book of activities, you can take on the world with assurance, style, and a healthy dose of silliness.

The best way to say goodbye is with some words of wisdom (and humor, of course). Take a deep breath and summon your inner hero when life throws you a curveball. Don't forget to call on Captain Calm and the Emotional Orchestra if you need help navigating the turbulent seas of emotion.

Feel free to share your thoughts and feelings with others; everyone's internal experiences are different. In times of turmoil, it is important to share both your happiness and your sadness with individuals you trust. The best treatment for stress is laughing, so keep that in mind whenever you need it. It may turn a gloomy day around and make people smile at each other.

Now set forth on your great journeys, my friends! Feel free to let your feelings explode like fireworks across the sky. Embrace the thrilling ups and downs of life, secure in the knowledge that you are in charge of your own mental health. And remember that you have a family of emotions here in this book, ready to help you whenever you need it; you are never alone.

As we end this journey, may you feel a surge of optimism, strength, and, yes, a little bit of silliness. Don't stop learning, developing, or letting go the incredible depths of your emotions. You, my dear friends, have the power to make the world a better and more hopeful place.

We appreciate your company on this amazing journey. Goodbye, but not really, because we'll definitely run into each other again in the wonderful world of "Emotions"!

Made in the USA
Las Vegas, NV
25 October 2023

79505318R10050